HIGHLIGHTS OF THE DENVER BRONCOS

MARYSA STORM

WORLD BOOK

BOLT

This World Book edition of *Highlights of the Denver Broncos* is published by agreement between Black Rabbit Books and World Book, Inc.
© 2019 Black Rabbit Books,
2140 Howard Dr. West,
North Mankato, MN 56003 U.S.A.
World Book, Inc.,
180 North LaSalle St., Suite 900,
Chicago, IL 60601 U.S.A.

Jennifer Besel, editor; Grant Gould & Michael Sellner, designers; Omay Ayres, photo researcher

Library of Congress Control Number: 2017044845

ISBN: 978-0-7166-3476-8

Printed in China. 3/18

CONTENTS

CHAPTER 1

On the FIELD

It was 1978. The Denver Broncos faced off against the Oakland Raiders. The winner would go to the Super Bowl. The Broncos played to win. **Receivers** made big catches. **Defenders** took down Raiders. The team won 20–17. And the crowd went wild. The Broncos would go to its first ever Super Bowl!

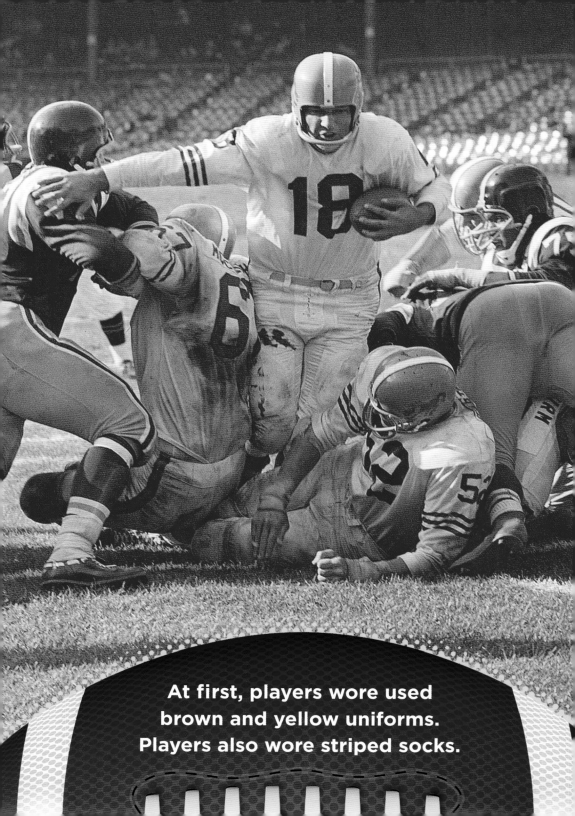

At first, players wore used brown and yellow uniforms. Players also wore striped socks.

CHAPTER 2

HISTORY
of the Broncos

The Broncos is a powerful team. But it didn't start that way. The team played its first game in 1960. It didn't have a winning season until 1973. Finally, it won more games than it lost. The team's coach, John Ralston, became **AFC** Coach of the Year.

Road to the Super Bowl

In 1978, the team went to its first Super Bowl. It lost by 17 points. The team lost the Super Bowl again in 1987, 1988, and 1990. It seemed the Broncos would never win the big game. That changed in 1998. At long last, the team won a Super Bowl.

Broncos' Super Bowl Timeline

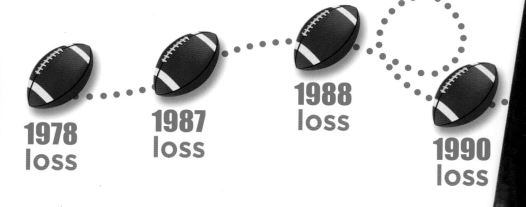

1978 loss

1987 loss

1988 loss

1990 loss

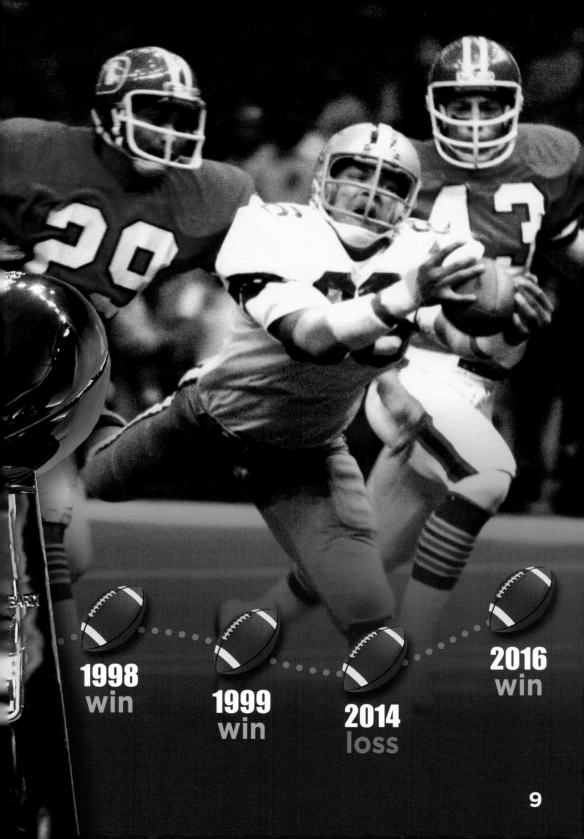

1998 win

1999 win

2014 loss

2016 win

One of the Broncos'
mascots is a live horse
named Thunder.

CHAPTER 3

Greatest MOMENTS

The Broncos' biggest moments have become incredible stories. Fans will never forget these games.

Five minutes of the 1986 AFC Championship remained. The Broncos were down seven points. Players stood 98 yards from a touchdown. The situation didn't look good. But players ran and passed the ball down the field. It took the team 15 **plays**, but it scored. The team won in overtime.

1998 Super Bowl

In 1998, the Broncos played its fifth Super Bowl. And this time, the team won. It beat the Green Bay Packers 31–24. Running back Terrell Davis made three touchdowns. Only five other players have made that many in one Super Bowl.

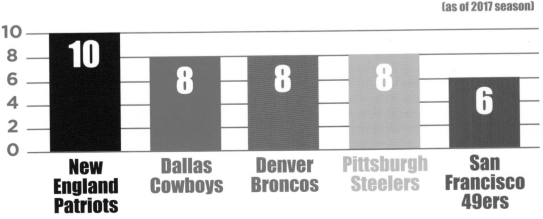

Most Super Bowl Appearances
(as of 2017 season)

	Appearances
New England Patriots	10
Dallas Cowboys	8
Denver Broncos	8
Pittsburgh Steelers	8
San Francisco 49ers	6

13

BY THE NUMBERS

64 yards

NFL's longest field goal (kicked by Bronco Matt Prater)

5

number of Super Bowl losses

606

all-time most points scored in a single season (earned by the 2013 Broncos)

44

Broncos' team record for most consecutive games with a touchdown pass (held by Peyton Manning)

CHAPTER 4

STARS
of the Broncos

Many great players have worn Broncos' jerseys. Fans consider running back Terrell Davis one of the team's greatest players. His speed and strength helped it win many games. Davis was **MVP** of the 1998 Super Bowl. He was also a two-time offensive player of the year.

During the 1998 Super Bowl, Davis had a migraine. It was so bad, he couldn't see. The coach sent him on the field anyway.

17

Orange Crush Defense

The Broncos' 1977 defense dominated. Fans called it the Orange Crush. The nickname came from the players' orange jerseys. With this powerful defense, the Broncos won the conference championship.

The Orange Crush's
1977 Stats

averaged 10.6 points allowed per game

only allowed 18 touchdowns in 14 regular-season games

- ranked 3rd in points allowed

Quarterbacks with Most Touchdown Passes

539 Peyton Manning (as of 2017 regular season)

508 Brett Favre

488 Drew Brees

488 Tom Brady

Peyton Manning

In 2012, Peyton Manning joined the Broncos. In 2016, he led the team to its third Super Bowl win. People call him one of the greatest quarterbacks. As of 2017, he still leads in all-time touchdown passes.

John Elway

For 16 seasons, quarterback John Elway led the Broncos. He played five Super Bowls with the team. Despite three Super Bowl losses, he never gave up. He always pushed the team on.

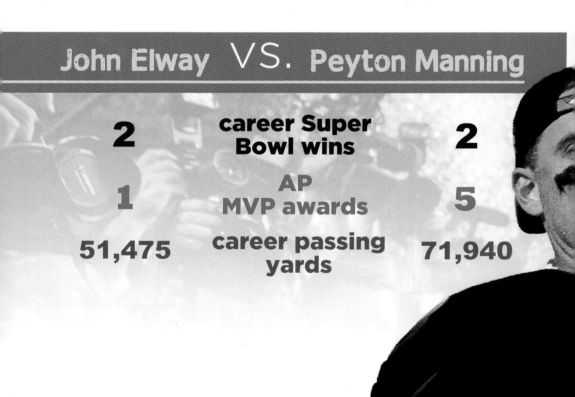

John Elway	VS. Peyton Manning	
2	career Super Bowl wins	2
1	AP MVP awards	5
51,475	career passing yards	71,940

23

Shannon Sharpe

Shannon Sharpe played as a Broncos' tight end. Fans knew him for his speed. He made many amazing **receptions**. Sharpe **retired** with more catches than any other tight end. He had more touchdowns and yards too.

Von Miller

Von Miller plays linebacker. He helped the Broncos' 2015 defense rank first over all. He also helped the team win the 2016 Super Bowl. Miller became the game's MVP. He is the 10th defensive player to get the award.

From a tough beginning to big wins, fans have stuck with the Broncos. They can't wait to see what this team does next.

Miller joined the Pro Bowl his **rookie** season. Only one other Bronco had done that before.

TIMELINE

1955

1960
Broncos play
first season.

1973
Team has first
winning season.

1977
Orange Crush
defense dominates.

1983
Elway joins
the Broncos.

1995
Team drafts Davis.

2004
Elway enters Pro Football Hall of Fame.

2016
Team wins third Super Bowl.

1998
Team wins first Super Bowl.

2012
Manning joins Broncos.

2017
Davis enters Pro Football Hall of Fame.

2020

AFC—American Football Conference; the AFC is one of two groups, which includes 16 teams, that make up the NFL (National Football League).

defender (de-FEN-dur)—a player who works to stop the other team from scoring

migraine (MI-grayn)—a severe headache

MVP—an award given to the best player in the league each season; MVP stands for most valuable player.

play (PLAY)—a planned action taken in a game

receiver (reh-SEE-vur)—a football player who catches passes thrown by the quarterback

reception (ree-SEP-shun)—catching a pass thrown toward the opponent's goal

retire (ree-TIYR)—to stop playing a game or competition

rookie (ROOK-ee)—a first-year player

BOOKS

Fishman, Jon M. *Von Miller.* Sports All-Stars. Minneapolis: Lerner Publications, 2018.

Kelley, Patrick. *Denver Broncos.* NFL Up Close. Minneapolis: Abdo Pub., 2016.

Morey, Allan. *The Denver Broncos Story.* NFL Teams. Minneapolis: Bellwether Media, Inc., 2017.

WEBSITES

Football: National Football League
www.ducksters.com/sports/national_football_league.php

NFL RUSH
www.nflrush.com

Official Site of the Denver Broncos
www.denverbroncos.com

INDEX